She is My Dream

Poems

By
Theron J. Parker

The Poetry She Inspired In Me

Dedication

Chen Meilian

Thank you for your inspiration

Acknowledgement

To all my friends,
Love is possible if you open your hearts.
To the Men and Women who serve and protect our great Country
To my brother Kelvin Parker
I am happy you found love.

Preface

Poetry is used to convey a simple to a deeper meaning of how a person feels. I have felt love and experienced the joy of love for another person. This experience has made me realize that love is the greatest gift that can be shared between two or more people. Poetry is a joy that takes the mind on a wonderful ride through life's wonderful and painful experiences. Poetry has existed from the first moment two people looked into each other's eyes and felt the spark of love. As a result, their hearts were commanded to speak the words "I love you" to one another. With this simple expression, the feeling of poetry was born.

Contents

Life Without You

What would I do if there were no tomorrow?

What if I opened my eyes and you were no longer there?

How could I possibly go forward

without being in your care?

What would happen to our friendship?

Would it simply dissipate?

Who will come and comfort me?

Who would cure my heartache?

What will life be without you?

A pain I could not bear.

It took so long to find you,

after I had searched for you everywhere.

Do you know what love is

Do you know what love is?
Can you feel it in your bones?
Do you know what love is?
Are you sad when you are alone?
Do you know what love is?
Can you speak it by its name?
Do you know what love is?
Will it always be the same?
Do you know what love is?
Does it come from the sky?
Is it a gift that he gives?
The man who lives on high.

You

In every town and village,
in every city square.
In crowded places
I searched the faces,
hoping to find someone to care.
Then you came into my life
like a promised sunrise.
You brighten my days
with the light in your eyes.
Now, I will always be strong.
I have your friendship,
I will never be alone.

Cup of Tea

You are my cup of tea.
Come closer to my face.
I want to enjoy you,
Just sipping the whole day.
My love,
I cannot deny it.
You are sweeter than sugar,
And Mom's apple pie.

The Sun and Her

She stands in the light of the day.
The sun's rays form a backdrop
for her magnificent beauty.
The sky opens up just enough,
allowing a rainbow to come from the heavens.
Her smile warms the air
as birds dance upon her breath.
She raises her arms and is lifted
by the sun's rays for all to see.
Her presence beautifies life itself
as she stands in the light of the sun.

The Flower in the Garden

The sun awakens early each morning.
He wants to be the first to see her rise.
He rubs his hands together gently.
Warming the air just enough to awaken her petals.
The sun absorbed the moisture,
Left by the early morning dew.
All the garden creatures encircle her
As she stands tall and looks brilliant
in the presence of the sun.
She stretches forth her arms,
so all may see,
the beautiful flower in the garden.

Thinking of You

Today is like yesterday
and many days before.
I have no control over my thoughts
and the smile that appears on my face.
Each time I think of you,
my happiness takes on a new meaning.

Friends

I know
I only asked to be your friend.
But your beauty
has affected my emotions within.
So, please accept each poem
that I send
as a token of friendship
between a female
and her male friend.

If Time Stood Still

If time stood still for just one day?
Think of what we could do.
As we went on our way.
I could send you flowers one at a time or in a bunch.
We could go to your favorite restaurant,
sit down, and have lunch.
What a joy it would be to go to a play.
When it ended,
we could be together for the rest of the day.
If time stood still for just one day,
Mother Nature and
Father Time
would be in love the same way.

Tomorrow

If tomorrow were my heart, I needed to give,
It would be yours for as long as you live.
If tomorrow were my eyes that you needed to see,
I would give them up freely to you from me.
If tomorrow were my love, you needed to feel,
I would give up my life so you could live.
All my love to you, I would give
If tomorrow were forever,
and forever you could live.

Love

I sat silently on a bench.

Looking out into a green meadow,

I watched the sun's rays cutting through the trees.

I stared out into the distance,

I felt the beat of my heart increase

with each thought of you.

In my dream

In my dream,
I am not alone.
I see happiness,
and I see you.

The Fourteenth Day

My eyes opened, and I looked
out into the early morning dawn.
I thought of the dream I had during the night
and the feelings that stirred within me.
Many images linger in my mind.
I can recall the moment.
It was the fourteenth day that I found you.

Felt

I have never felt your touch,
but I have felt the joy of life
that flows through you.

Poetry Comes From You

My heart exploded with joy.
I saw heaven open up before me.
I beheld your beauty,
and happiness will carry the day.
It is amazing how you move me.
All the beautiful thoughts in my mind.
Can it be that poetry comes from you?

I am moved

From the first time I heard your voice,
I have been waiting for our first meeting.
I do not know why I am moved,
but I am moved by you.

My Heart Was Crying During the Night

My heart was crying during the night.
It made me reach for the phone,
To text you the words before they are all gone.
My heart was crying throughout the night,
I wonder if you heard the sound
of love dancing in the air
and bouncing all around.
To call you up, I would not dare.
Our love was spreading everywhere.

Sip

I wish I had one night
To sip a glass of wine with you.
We would enjoy our friendship for hours,
Until the bottle is made new.

Image

I looked at your image, and it is captivating.
I feel the warmth of your spirit,
communicating with me.
Looking at your image,
I imagine being held in your arms.
I looked at your image,
knowing
I could love you forever.

Friendship

What is a perfect friendship
that I only think of you?
Why are you always on my mind?
Are you a gift given at the right time?
What is friendship
but the gift that you give?
I hope to be your friend
for as long as we both shall live.

Can I

Can I love you
in my own little way?
Can my heart withstand the pain
of not seeing you every day?
Can I love you and stay the same,
or will I lose you,
and my mind goes insane?

Waiting

I am waiting
on the first touch of your hand.
I am waiting
to see the smile on your face.
I am waiting
for that unforgettable moment
that will last me
for the rest of my days.

Your Lips, Your Eyes, Your Smile

Your lips are so beautiful.
They bring beauty to your face.
Your lips define you.
They are filled with love, charm, and grace.
Your eyes are so perfect.
They give joy to your life each day.
They are centered to show kindness,
as I look upon your face.
Your smile is so majestic.
When I look at you, I know you care.
And on each day, I greet you
Love will be sent everywhere.

You are My Sunshine

You are my Sunshine.
You are the light of my day.
Your love warms me
as I go about my way.

I know

I know we have never kissed.
We have never held each other's hands.
I know we have only spoken a few times
but I still want to be your man.
We have never sat down and had a meal.
We have never done anything at all.
At night, I would love to be your pillow.
To catch your head when you fall.
I have never seen a morning sun
that looks as beautiful as you.
To see it set in the evening
I will feel happiness through and through.
I may never walk you down the aisle
or stand up and say I do.
But I confess with all my heart,
I really do love you.

On This Day

On this day,
I will cry one single tear.
It will mark the day
my love flourished for you.
Forever,
my heart will be sealed in its case.
No other love
will come and take your place.
For all eternity,
my love will stand.
It will be a testament
to how much love
a woman
can receive from a man.

One Night

One night with you,
will I survive?
Will I melt in your hands
from the look in your eyes?
One night with you,
seduced by your charm,
lying beside you,
wrapped in your arms.
One night with you
is the way love should be.
Madly in love for all eternity.

I Want to Be That Man

I want to be that man
who wakes you up each morning.
The man who gives you the sweetest kiss
and puts a smile of happiness on your face.

I want to be that man
who cooks you breakfast
and prepare you for your day.
The man who gives you love
as we both go out on our own way.

I want to be that man
who closes the curtain at night.
Preparing for that private moment
when we hold each other tight.

I Want to Be That Man Cont.

I want to be that man,
who combs your hair after you shower.
The man who blows each strand of hair dry,
even if it takes hours.

I want to be that man,
who looks deep into your eyes.
That man who kisses you with so much passion,
that you will moan with surprise.

I want to be that man,
who gives you his touch in the proper way,
that you feel the true meaning of desire,
happiness, love, and intimacy,
and you will always want to stay.
Lastly, I want to be the man,
who gives you all the love you have created in me.

The Letter

She is more desirable
than all the riches of the world.
She is in my every thought
and all my dreams.
She is more pleasing to the eye
than a polished diamond.
She is
Her lips look like a rose petal
from a fresh morning blossom.
Her skin looks as smooth
as silk spun in the moonlight.
Her hair moves slowly
as if kissed by a summer breeze.
She is my rising sun and my sunset.
She is

Crab Legs

I was lying in the ocean,
and someone put me in a sack.
Later that day, I heard a big crack.
Off came my legs, and I was tossed in a pot.
There, I stayed until the water was hot.
Twenty minutes later, I was displayed on a plate.
I asked the man why.
He said they liked eating me that way.

Hot Pot

Along with you,
there I am not.
You are sitting with friends,
enjoying Hot Pot.
In the future,
I hope it will be.
You will be at my table
eating hot pot with me.

She

She touched my heart
with a simple hello.
She said I missed you
with her smile.
Her eyes said meeting you
will be the start of eternal happiness.

Can I Kiss You

Can I kiss you below your neck?
It will include your breasts, shoulders, and arms.
Can I kiss you below your waist?
I promise it will be in good taste.
Can I kiss you on that spot?
You know,
the spot that Mother Nature made hot.
All these kisses will add up to one.
It is that first kiss where love comes from.

The Seed

The seed of happiness is in all of us.
From a little child, it grows.
The seed of love calls out
as we search for that perfect mate.
But the seed of truth always leads us
down many roads to uncertainty.

I

I stand in the darkness alone.
I listen to the anger around me.
But I can still see the beauty of the storm.

Truth

My truth is for me to know
and you to learn.
Your truth is for you to know
and for me to yearn.

I see

What do I see when I look at you?
I see joy flowing through your soul.
It is the reason that you are whole.

What do I see when I look at you?
I see happiness upon your crown.
You have a desire to enjoy life.
You do not slow down.

What do I see when I look at you?
I see a woman who no one can measure.
I see a woman who walks at her own pace.
I see a woman whom I can treasure.

When We Make Love

When we make love
I will look into your eyes.
I will hold you close as we begin the ride.
I will kiss your lips,
and press my body firmly
to your breast.
I will make little noises
as your hand strokes my chest.
My lips will summon
your desire inside.
We will both
become victims
of the ultimate prize.
When we make love, it will be
exhilarating, you will see.
I know the joy of this union
will be the love
you give to me.

When We Make Love Part II

When we make love
I will feel your body heat.
I will give you my love
from your head to your feet.
First, touching your breast
with my lips and my tongue,
then kissing the rest
till your pleasure is sung.
It will be ecstasy
into the center of your soul.
I will greet you deeply
until you are whole.
A sound you will make.
You will have to declare
as we explode in ecstasy
our love will flow everywhere.

Dare To Dream

Dare I think it is possible?
Dare I love you
And never kiss your lips?
Do I dare become a part of you
so that we can exist as one?

Candy

I want to take my time with you.

You look ever so sweet.

I want to be ready.

No matter what day we meet.

I want to take off your wrapper,

one piece at a time.

I want you to look at me,

so that you know you are mine.

I will pull your soft body up to my lips.

You are in the shape of a woman,

I would start at your hips.

Do not be afraid as you join with my tongue.

Just relax and enjoy; we are about to have fun.

So, as you lie there, consumed by my mouth.

Remember, its sole purpose is to make you cry out.

Now, just before the session would end,

I would unwrap you.

To taste your sweetness,

again and again.

My Destiny

Can I find true love,
within the comfort of your arms?
Will this road I have traveled,
give me the love I seek.
Is your appearance in my life leading me,
to happiness and peace?
Can it be that meeting you,
will be my destiny?

My Pearl

I want to sit before you
and say the magic words.
I want to touch you in a way
that you will freely open up
and give me what is inside.
I want to explore your softness,
revealing what you have taken
a long time to make.
My pearl.

Desire

Yes, I have a desire for your every touch.
I want to kneel before you.
I will not beg that much.
Yes, I have a desire.
You know I will plead.
I will plead for your love.
From your head to your knees.
Yes, I desire to be at the peak of your seat.
Do not worry about me.
I pass every challenge I meet.

Love's Destiny

I stand on top of a mountain.

The morning fog obscures the valley below.

I cannot see the image

traveling along the road.

But I know she will come for me.

I can hear the beat of her heart.

With every step she takes.

At the end of her travels.

I will, at long last.

Receive love's destiny.

Good morning

If I were your man.
"Good morning,"
would be the first words.
You would hear each day.
The next words would be,
"I love you so much."

Good Night

If I were your man.
I would kiss you goodnight.
With my heart beating in rhythm.
I would hold you so tight.
And as we lie down.
Before we go to sleep.
I would give you all the love.
That you would all need.
I would tell you I love you.
Just one more time.
Then I would give thanks.
"To God," the Father.
That you were all mine.

Making Love

Making love to you,
where would I start?
Will I tell you I love you,
and it comes from my heart?
Would I kiss you
passionately on your lips?
I must admit I am partial
to what lies between your hips.
What instructions would you give me,
as I look into your eyes?
Or would you lie there,
wanting to be surprised?
As I take my time from your head
to your feet.
The explosion you receive,
will it be ever so sweet?
Yes, making love to you
would be one of a kind.
At the end of our session
I know you will be mine.

Sharing a Meal With You

I long for the day when we
sit down to eat.
I can see how beautiful it will be.
The lights are dim, and you are beautiful.
I am happy to be with you.
The waiter knew just what to bring.
A seafood medley of your favorite foods.
We have a glass of room-temperature water.
To wash down our anticipation.
A salad is first given
with different lettuces,
spring, baby, and cress.
The house dressing is delicious to the taste.
Now comes the first serving.
The crab legs are enormous.
Where in the world did they come from?
I think they came from deep in the Bering Sea.
The squid is cooked to perfection.

Sharing a Meal With You (Cont)

They are both fried and boiled.
The mussels are prepared in a curry sauce.
My mouth is jumping for joy.
The salmon is pan-fried.
And displayed on a bed of white rice.
My mouth is watering.
We are ready to consume
each item lying before us.
Yes, sharing a meal with you
It is a dream come true.
I hope we can enjoy it all
before the night is through.

A Love Letter

Oddly, you have affected me so romantically. I'm glad I was introduced to you. When I saw you, I fell in love. I realize that I briefly held your hand and kissed your lips. But I love how you have allowed me to become close to you romantically. You have a good spirit. We all started on our paths in life, meeting different people along the way. I like you very much. No, I love you very much. I know you understand what I mean. So, my beautiful lady, thank you for allowing me to express how you make me feel and for letting me shower you with love and affection every day. And in the end, if we remain apart, I want you to know that my love for you will never die. I will put it in a box in my heart that only you can claim.

Swallow-tailed Bird

You are the symbol of a beautiful bird.
Your beauty is majestic upon sight.
With every movement that you make.
All adore you while you are in flight.
Even though you do not take to the air.
Your presence reveals your love and care.
You bring balance, freedom, happiness, and hope.
With intelligence, perseverance, transformation, and love.
A gift to all who serve him from above.
Yan, you are my gift, my little Swallow-Tail Bird.

Through My Eyes

Through my eyes,
let me show you love.
Look into my heart
and you can see your love
flowing inside of me.

Through my eyes,
you can see the exact moment
when I first received the thought
to say I love you.

I Don't Want to Be Caught

I don't want to be caught.
I know that she is up there.
I don't want to look up and see her eyes.
She will take us all by surprise.
I don't want to be caught.
I am just a crab.
I want to keep my legs.
Offer her some shrimp.
Lobster and vegetables instead.
Return me to the Bering Sea.
That is the best place for me to be.

A Love Letter to Meilian II

Good morning, my beautiful Meilian.

I am happy every day just because I am privileged to know you.

I look forward to saying good morning and good night

to you daily.

It is the gift of friendship that you have shared with me. All day long, I think of words to put in a poem to express how special you are to me. So, when I say I love you. I truly appreciate how you have allowed me to be a part of your incredible existence. I look at your videos and photos and fall madly in love with you. You are one in a million ladies who can make people want to be a part of your life. So, my poem for you today is simple.

"Poem"

I love you because you are beautiful.

I love you because you are kind.

I love you because of the love you give to me.

Thank You

Thank You.
I was drowning in my tears.
I was feeling the pain of lost love.
I was feeling the agony of living.

Thank you for looking into my heart
and reading the words of excitement,
my words of happiness, hope, and joy.

Thank you for allowing me
to glimpse what it could be like
to give you my love.
To experience
how a man could feel a
rebirth in spirit,
and know that
there is still love in all of us.
Thank you.

Catching My Breath

I find it hard
to catch this feeling that belongs to me.
It is as complicated as it seems.
She must be the one,
when I share my emotions.
I can feel my breath escaping.
How can I become whole?
I must take charge,
and stay in sync with her.

Catching my breath.
My life flashes before my eyes.
It is in that moment.
When you have given.
A unique gift to be part of creation.

Today

Today, I sit and think of your
friendship, your sense of humor,
and the way you let me know you like me.
You send me a joke now and then.
You show me your wisdom in each video,
which you had shared with me.
I know you desire to let me enjoy who you are.
You take me to lunch and dinner.
You allow me to meet your friends.
Even though I am miles away.
Maybe one day I can look you in the eyes
and say it in a poem.
"I do love,
I do need,
and I do wish"
After we make love.
Wake me up in the morning,
and I can tell you more.

Hands

Are you okay?
A sexy voice asked from the room.
Her hands are soft, smooth, yet firm.
Each finger finds its proper place.
I relax and let the softness of her hands.
Take my breath away.

The Wind and My Sweet Swallow-Tail

I am the wind.
I form beautiful landscapes in nature.
I move the clouds from one place to the next.
I carry the bird's songs far and wide.
I am the wind, my sweet Swallow-tail.
Come dance with me.
And sing your song for all to hear.
Oh, my sweet Swallow-Tail.
You are my greatest delight.

One Second

Just one second,
is all I need
to tell you
I am yours
for all eternity.

Just Before Tomorrow

Just before tomorrow.
My heart beats too fast.
My mind races out of control.

Just before tomorrow.
I think of your eyes.
Receiving my looks.
I have a desire to caress you.
I have a need to say.
I love you so
Very much.

Leaving Too Soon

Leaving too soon,
it was when my heart began to ache.
I will wait to be with you again,
no matter how long it takes.

Flying South

As you fly south, my beautiful Bird.
Remember the love you carry with you.
As you arrive in the Atlantic winds.
Keep your memories of me close.
I am only a heartbeat away.

Feeling Alive

The smell of the water in the bay.
The view of the sun shining brightly
upon the ocean waves.
The sound of the birds singing
and the thought of you next to me.
I feel alive with you.

Can I Say it (Song)

Can I say it in a poem?
Your kindness, your smile, your touch,
and your warmth
makes a wonderful day.
When I am in your arms,
all my sadness and pain go away.

Can I say it in a song so you can hear,
that you take away all my fears.
I love to hear you say
in your sweet and loving way.
Is it as good for you as it is for me?

So, can I say it in a poem?
It will not take very long.
Or shall I sing it in a song for you to hear?
Is it as good for you as it is for me?

Can I Sleep With You Tonight (Song)

Can I sleep with you tonight?
I don't care
whether it's right or wrong.
I need you in my arms.
I need to feel your love,
and feel your warmth.

Can you please hold me tight?
Can you help me
make it through the night?
I want to put the past behind me.
I want to tell you what's on my mind.
Know our love will always last.
If we can forget about the past.

Tomorrow may never come.
All this love, I know where it is from.
So please hold me tight.
We can make it through the night.

Can I Sleep with You Tonight (Song Cont.)

It doesn't matter whether we are wrong or right.

Baby, hold me in your arms.

Let me feel all your love and warmth.

Maybe tomorrow will be a brighter day.

Baby, hold me in your arms.

Let me feel all your warmth.

Can I sleep with you tonight?

Fun Together (Song)

We can have some fun together.
This is the perfect weather.
Even though your heart will not be in mind.
We don't have to waste this perfect time.

We can have some fun together.
We did not commit a crime.
I am yours, and you are mine.
Our bodies are both perfectly aligned.

We can have some fun together.
I will tell you what's on my mind.
We have an hour.
And that is fine.
When we started, it was close to nine.

Girl, you have blown my mind.
You are beautiful and divine.

Fun together (cont.)

We can have fun together.
No matter what is the weather.

Our bodies are both aligned.
We have to make good use of this time.
When we started, it was close to nine.
Girl, you really have blown my mind.
You are so beautiful and so dam fine.
Making love to you is on my mind.
We can have fun together.

Touch

My lips have felt the joy.
You offer a kind gift of happiness.
My hands have felt the fire.
You store inside your soul.
My eyes behold the pleasure you give me.
I sit alone, enjoying each beautiful moment.
As I think of your touch.

Hunger

My heart is on fire.

My mind yearns for satisfaction.

My stomach is in knots.

I hunger for your touch, your breath upon my lips.

I hunger for your words to speak to me.

I hunger for that exact moment.

That takes our emotions to the ultimate climax.

I hunger for you.

Darkness Comes

Darkness comes, and our eyes see a different life.
The life we have, the life we want, and the life we love.
Tonight, I give you the life I have.
It is an empty shell without you.
Tonight, I also give you the life I want.
It is filled with memories of you.
And tonight, I give you the life I love.
It is the love I have shared with you.
Lips to lips, eyes to eyes, body to body,
and heart to heart.
When darkness comes, I only think of you.

My Beautiful Friend

The sun is shining bright,
spreading joy everywhere.
The thoughts of our meeting,
make this a beautiful day.
You are like a flower,
being kissed by the morning sun.

If I Would Die Tomorrow

If I were to die tomorrow.
I would not have a single regret.
I have lived a lifetime of love.
Starting with the day we first met.
I have known the feels of true love.
And the soul in which it resides.
I have given all my heart.
Before the day I did expire.

If I were to die tomorrow.
Remember the love we once shared.
It will tell the story of two people.
And how much they did care.

If I were to die tomorrow.
Have no sorrow about our love.
We were granted one special moment.
It was a gift from God above.

She is My Dream

Part I

I first saw her while I was having lunch with a friend.

It was only for a few seconds.

Who was this delightful woman I had met?

I saw her in her first video; she was on a plane.

I sat there watching and enjoying the moment.

I could see her happiness with her friends.

Part II

I saw her in her second video, and she was on a merry-go-round.

The wind blew lightly, dancing with her hair.

She was having fun.

I thought to myself.

She is the most beautiful woman on the face of the earth.

She is my dream.

She is My Dream (cont)

Part III

Now, I send her poetry each day.

Just as a friend, could she come my way?

The subsequent communications.

The photos were sent to me one at a time.

I slept in my bed with dreams in my mind.

She is my dream.

Part IV

I was lonely all day; the phone did not ring.

I sent her a poem, a simple one, it seemed.

She sent another video of her riding in a car.

She was returning from having a meal with her friends.

They didn't drive far.

So, all day long, it seemed like a week.

She sent me the ultimate videos that were ever so sweet.

She was on a beach having a good time.

It was addressed to me by my friend on Valentine.

汉译诗**特集**

一封情书

很高兴有人介绍我认识你。说来也怪，你竟然如此浪漫地触动了我。初见你，我就爱上了你。我知道，我只不过握过你的手，轻轻地吻过你的唇。但我爱你让我如此亲近你。你拥有美好的精神。你和我，从不同的人生轨迹开始，一路上结识了不同的人。我必须承认，我非常喜欢你。不，我非常爱你。我知道你明白我的意思。所以，我美丽的女士，谢谢你允许我表达你的感受，谢谢你让我每天都倾注爱与关怀。最后，即使我们永远分开，我想让你知道，我对你的爱永不消逝。我会永远把你的爱放在心上。

没有你的生活

如果没有明天我会做什么？

如果我睁开眼睛，你却不再存在，那该怎么办？

我怎么可能继续前进

而没有受到你的照顾？

我们的友谊会怎样？

它会就此消散吗？

谁会来安慰我？

我的心痛谁来治愈？

如果没有你，生活将会怎样？

我无法忍受的痛苦。

花了这么长时间才找到你，

我到处寻找你。

你知道爱是什么吗

你知道什么是爱吗？

你能从骨子里感受到它吗？

你知道什么是爱吗？

当你孤独的时候，你会难过吗？

你知道什么是爱吗？

你能说出它的名字吗？

你知道什么是爱吗？

它会一直一样吗？

你知道什么是爱吗？

它是从天上来的吗？

这是他送的礼物吗？

住在高处的人。

一杯茶

你是我的菜。

靠近我的脸。

我想享受你，

整天都在喝。

亲爱的，

我无法否认这一点。

你比糖还甜，

还有妈妈的苹果派。

如果时间静止

如果时间只停留一天呢？

想想我们能做什么。

我们继续前行。

我可以一次送你一朵花，也可以送你一束花。

我们可以去你最喜欢的餐厅，

坐下来吃午饭。

去看一场戏是多么快乐的事情啊。

当一切结束时，

我们可以在一起度过这一天的剩余时间。

如果时间静止一天，

大自然和

时间之父

也会以同样的方式坠入爱河。

明天

如果明天是我的心，我需要给予，

只要你活着，它就永远属于你。

如果明天是我的眼睛，你需要看到，

我愿意免费把它们送给你。

如果明天是我的爱，你需要感受，

为了让你活下去，我愿意放弃我的生命。

我愿意把我所有的爱都给你

如果明天是永远

你将永远活下去。

你的嘴唇，你的眼睛，你的微笑

你的嘴唇真漂亮。

它们给你的脸庞带来美丽。

你的嘴唇定义了你。

他们充满爱、魅力和优雅。

你的眼睛真完美。

它们给你每天的生活带来欢乐。

他们以展现善意为中心，

当我看着你的脸。

你的笑容如此美丽。

当我看着你时，我知道你在乎。

每天我都会问候你

爱将传递到世界各地。

在这一天

这一天，

我将流下一滴眼泪。

这将标志着这一天

我对你的爱日益浓烈。

永远，

我的心将被封存在盒子里。

没有其他的爱

将会来代替你。

永恒不变，

我的爱将永存。

这将是一份遗嘱

有多少爱

一名女性

可以从男人那里得到。

这封信

她更受欢迎

比世界上所有的财富都多。

我心里想的都是她

以及我所有的梦想。

她更赏心悦目

比抛光钻石还要坚硬。

她是

她的嘴唇看起来像玫瑰花瓣

来自一朵新鲜的早晨的花朵。

她的皮肤看起来很光滑

如同月光下纺出的丝绸。

她的头发慢慢地飘动

仿佛被夏日微风亲吻。

她是我的朝阳，也是我的夕阳。

她是

做爱

和你做爱。

我该从哪里开始呢？

我会告诉你我爱你吗

这是发自内心的吗？

我会吻你吗

热情地吻上你的嘴唇？

我必须承认我有偏见

到你臀部之间的东西。

你会给我什么指示

当我看着你的眼睛时？

或者你会躺在那里？

想要得到惊喜。

当我从你的脑海里抽出时间时

到你的脚边。

你收到的爆炸

将会非常甜蜜。

是的，和你做爱

将是独一无二的。

在我们会议结束时

我知道你会是我的。

Previous Literary Works

By

Theron J. Parker

Novels

Beijing

It is Because of You That I Know How to Love

Road to Two Hearts

Poetry

Poems Inspired by Kelly

Poems from the Heart

Visions of True Love

Children Books

June Bug and The Country Toys

June Bug and the Roll-A-Packer

Contribution made to

"Grandma and The Grapefruit Tree"

By Chunhong Li

www.ingramcontent.com/pod-product-compliance
Lightning Source LLC
Chambersburg PA
CBHW051225120626
46547CB00013B/1518